Old Gold.
Gold in the Ancient World

by Donna Latham

Editorial Offices: Glenview, Illinois • Parsippany, New Jersey • New York, New York
Sales Offices: Needham, Massachusetts • Duluth, Georgia • Glenview, Illinois
Coppell, Texas • Ontario, California • Mesa, Arizona

Every effort has been made to secure permission and provide appropriate credit for photographic material. The publisher deeply regrets any omission and pledges to correct errors called to its attention in subsequent editions.

Unless otherwise acknowledged, all photographs are the property of Scott Foresman, a division of Pearson Education.

Photo locators denoted as follows: Top (T), Center (C), Bottom (B), Left (L), Right (R), Background (Bkgd)

Opener ©Lois Ellen Frank/CORBIS; 1 ©Bettmann/CORBIS; 3 © Charles O'Rear/CORBIS; 4 ©Michael S. Lewis/CORBIS; 5 ©Dan Lamont/CORBIS; 6 ©Bettmann/CORBIS; 7 ©Bettmann/CORBIS; 9(T) ©Araldo de Luca/CORBIS; 9(B) ©Araldo de Luca/CORBIS; 10 ©Elio Ciol/CORBIS; 11 ©Araldo de Luca/CORBIS; 12 ©Araldo de Luca/CORBIS; 13 ©Stapleton Collection/CORBIS; 14 ©Gianni Dagli Orti/CORBIS; 15 ©Archivo Iconografico, S.A./CORBIS; 16 ©Gian Berto Vanni/CORBIS; 17 ©Gianni Dagli Orti/CORBIS; 18 ©Reuters/CORBIS; 19 ©Corbis; 20 ©Sucheta Das/Reuters/Corbis; 21 © Lois Ellen Frank/CORBIS

ISBN: 0-328-13583-6

Copyright © Pearson Education, Inc.

All Rights Reserved. Printed in the United States of America. This publication is protected by Copyright, and permission should be obtained from the publisher prior to any prohibited reproduction, storage in a retrieval system, or transmission in any form by any means, electronic, mechanical, photocopying, recording, or likewise. For information regarding permission(s), write to: Permissions Department, Scott Foresman, 1900 East Lake Avenue, Glenview, Illinois 60025.

7 8 9 10 V0G1 14 13 12 11 10 09 08

A PRECIOUS METAL

Gold is a **precious** metal. It is rare and worth a lot of money. Both soft and heavy, gold can be pounded, pushed, and formed into many different shapes. It can be flattened into sheets so thin, you can almost see through them. Yet, with all that pressing and flattening, gold won't break! Because it is so strong, many ancient gold objects are still around.

Heated to 2,192° F, molten gold is poured into special containers.

A gold miner drills in a shaft in a gold mine.

A gold mine in the Mojave Desert

Gold was one of the first metals found. It was discovered about five thousand years ago. Many people wanted this dazzling treasure. People searched for gold. They mined and traded it. They melted it into coins and used it to **adorn** themselves with crowns, rings, and bracelets.

WHERE IS GOLD FOUND?

For many ancient cultures, gold meant power and wealth. Rulers sent troops out of their **realms** to find gold in other kingdoms. Gold is found in soil, rocks, riverbeds, and the ocean. Most deposits of gold are deep in Earth's core.

Today gold mining is called lode mining. Gold lode deposits are found inside rocks. To remove these rocks from pits, miners drill into them.

King Midas's daughter is turned to gold.

ANCIENT GREECE

The ancient Greeks believed that gold was magical. In the myth of King Midas, Midas asked the gods for the golden touch. Everything he touched turned to gold, including his daughter! Seeing her **lifeless** golden form taught him a lesson. Only when he was able to **cleanse** himself of greed did he lose this "gift." For him, it had become a curse. Today, we say someone who earns money easily has "the Midas touch."

Gold coins showing Alexander the Great were issued during his reign.

In ancient Greece, each town minted its own coins. When coins are minted, metal is stamped with certain marks. In Greece, most coins were made of copper or silver. Those metals were easier to find and less costly than gold. Only a few coins were made of gold.

Many think Alexander the Great (356-323 B.C.) was the greatest general who ever lived. He was crowned king of Macedonia when he was just twenty years old. His large empire included Persia, Egypt, and India.

Alexander standardized the money system throughout most of his empire. He used Persian gold to back the value of the gold coins he had minted. The standardization of the money system increased trade throughout the empire.

After Alexander's death, the Macedonian empire was broken up into separate kingdoms. Alexander's coins continued to be the standard for trade throughout most of his former lands for a long time after his death.

A gold laurel wreath

Alexander the Great

A gold and cameo bracelet with figures of Cupid, Athena, and Mercury

ANCIENT ROME

In ancient Rome, gold jewelry played a big part in daily life. Gold clasps were often used to hold togas together. Both common folks and high leaders wore togas, which were much like large sheets. Common people wore plain white togas. Leaders wore more costly ones that were made of finer materials. They were trimmed in purple and fastened with a gold brooch. Those who could not afford gold used pins made of bone.

Ancient gold earring with five pendants

In ancient Rome, a promise of marriage was sealed with a ring. This engagement ring was worn on the third finger of the left hand. Formed from gold, the ring showed two joined hands. This meant a promise. Today, engagement rings are still worn on the third finger of the left hand.

The Roman Empire was huge and powerful. It spread across continents. It included nearly half of Europe, parts of Africa, and a huge chunk of the Middle East. As the empire grew, trade became more important. To make coins for trade, the Roman Empire minted coins from bronze, silver, copper, and gold.

Ancient European gold ring with seated figure of a woman

A Roman wedding

A gold ornament of a figure worn against the chest by Aztec nobility or religious leaders

THE AZTECS

In the 1400s and early 1500s, the Aztec empire of Mexico was also powerful. The Aztecs lived in the Valley of Mexico. The valley did not have its own gold deposits, so the Aztecs demanded golden tribute from the regions they ruled.

In the Aztec culture, only the wealthy or the noble classes were allowed to wear gold. A ruler might wear a gold headband or armband.

The gods were very important to the Aztecs. Craftspeople made crowns and put them on statues of the gods.

When Spanish warriors conquered the Aztec empire in 1521, gold treasures were melted down and taken away. We do not know how many such gold artifacts were actually lost.

Portrait of Aztec emperor Montezuma II

A woman dressed in embroidered Inca costume at the carnival parade of Oruro, Bolivia

THE INCA

Like the Aztecs in Mexico, the Inca in South America built a powerful empire during the 1400s and early 1500s.

In the Inca culture, rules were harsh. Only the royalty could own gold and the state controlled all business and trade.

The sun god was very important to the Inca. People believed that their emperor was related to the sun god. They built temples and golden sun masks to honor this god. They believed that deposits of gold were "sweat from the sun."

The Inca were famous for their gold and their skill as craftspeople. They had rich lands with gold deposits in their streams. They would sift through sand at riverbanks to find gold. Even in a small **spoonful** of sand, a precious nugget might be hidden.

In the 1500s, conquering Spanish soldiers melted down much of the Inca gold art and jewelry and took it back to Spain.

This gold sun mask was probably worn as a head ornament.

GOLD AS A KEY TO THE PAST

A gold plaque, recently discovered off the coast of Alexandria, Egypt, is helping archaeologists solve a mystery from the past. The plaque is from the third century B.C. It bears an inscription confirming that the ancient site is the fabled lost city of Heracleion.

Heracleion is described in ancient texts as the gateway to the land of the pharaohs. It was once Egypt's main port and customs post. It was built long before Alexandria was founded in 331 B.C., and was famous through the ancient world.

An ancient Greek historian wrote that the city was named after the god Heracles. According to legend, Heracles saved the city from a flood of the Nile river.

Excavations have revealed that the city was the site of a magnificent temple to Amon, the supreme deity of the pharaohs. Many Egyptian rulers claimed to be Amon's descendants.

Heracleion was destroyed by a series of natural disasters, including earthquakes, and a possible sea-level rise or tidal wave. Today, the ruins of the city that was once Egypt's main port lie almost four miles from the coastline.

Deep layers of silt have covered and preserved carvings and colossal statues. Archaeologists have excavated only a tiny part of the city so far. The project could take decades to complete.

Although the gold plaque lay in seawater for more than a thousand years, it was still glistening on the seabed when it was found by divers!

GOLD TODAY

Gold is still considered a beautiful, precious metal that fills people with enchantment. Over the past twenty-five years, gold production has increased. Most of the world's gold is mined in South Africa. In the United States, Nevada is the main producer.

An Indian woman tries on gold jewelry for the Hindu festival of Dhanteras.

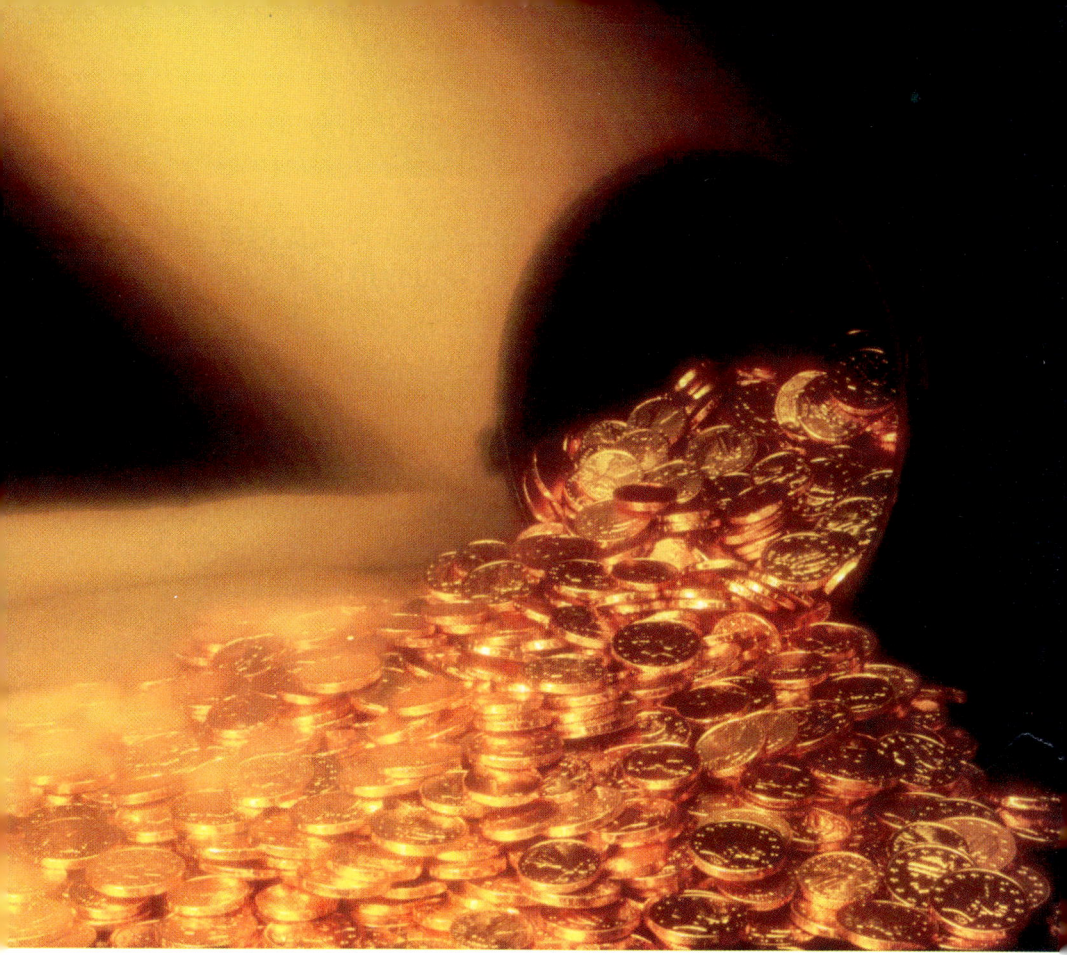

THE GOLDEN GLOW

You have learned about gold and its role in ancient cultures. You know how gold can be mined. You have read about the ways it was used to make jewelry, coins, and masks.

The golden glow of this tough and shiny metal has continued through history.

Glossary

adorn *v.* to decorate or add ornaments to.

cleanse *v.* to make pure.

lifeless *adj.* dead.

precious *adj.* rare and valuable.

realms *n.* kingdoms.

spoonful *n.* as much as a spoon can hold.